HOW TO SHARE YOUR FAITH

PART THREE OF THE DEVELOPING GIFTS AND SKILLS SERIES

DR. HENDRIK J VORSTER

CONTENTS

HOW TO SHARE YOUR FAITH

PART THREE OF THE DEVELOPING GIFTS AND SKILLS SERIES

-- Disciple Manual --

How to share your Faith
Part Three of the Developing Gifts and Skills Series
(Disciple Manual)
By Dr. Hendrik J. Vorster

For more copies and information please visit and write to us at: www.
churchplantinginstitute.com
resources@churchplantinginstitute.com

ISBN 978-1-955923-15-6

PART I

HOW TO SHARE YOUR FAITH

Part Three of the Developing Gifts and Skills Series

INTRODUCTION TO SHARING OUR FAITH

SESSION ONE

W e are all witnesses of what God has done in our lives. Our call is to testify and share this with others.

Jesus taught His Disciples *the Spiritual Discipline of* _____ when He first taught them on the mountain. He said to them that they were **Light** and **Salt** and that they should let their *"light so shine before others that they may see your good deeds and glorify your Father in Heaven."* This is a clear directive to be a witness, to be a Light to the World.

Witnessing requires a commitment to both be a _____
and _____

> *Matthew 5:13-16 (NIV)* [13] *"You are the salt of the earth. But if the salt loses its saltiness, how can it be made salty again? It is no longer good for anything, except to be thrown out and trampled underfoot.* [14] *"You are the light of the world. A town built on a hill cannot be hidden.* [15] *Neither do people light a lamp and put it under a bowl. Instead they put it on its stand, and it gives light to everyone in the house.* [16] *In the same way, let your light*

shine before others, that they may see your good deeds and
glorify your Father in heaven.""

To be a _____ means that we commit to go on public display as an example for others to see the *Light* of Christ shining brightly in our lives through the _____ they observe in and through our lives.

To be _____ requires us to live worthily, upholding the values of the Kingdom of God through our high-principled conduct. On the other hand, to be a witness also requires us to share the Word of God by mouth.

Witnessing requires a commitment to _____ the Good News.

During the parting moments before Jesus Ascended to Heaven, He gave His Disciples the "**Great _____.**" The Great Commission requires us to ____ out into the whole world and _____ the Good News about Jesus Christ and _____ them into obedient Followers of Jesus Christ.

> *Mark 16:15 (NIV) "15 He said to them, "Go into all the world and*
> *preach the gospel to all creation."*

> *Mark 16:20 (NIV) "20 Then the disciples went out and preached*
> *everywhere, and the Lord worked with them and confirmed his*
> *word by the signs that accompanied it."*

Witnessing requires a commitment to both _____ and
_____

Jesus not only requires His Followers to "*go into all the world and preach the gospel,*" but He also requires them to _____ those whose hearts are opened and who respond to the Gospel message that is preached.

> *Matthew 28:19-20 (NIV) "19 Therefore go and make disciples of all*
> *nations, baptizing them in the name of the Father and of the*
> *Son and of the Holy Spirit, 20 and teaching them to obey*
> *everything I have commanded you. And surely, I am with you*
> *always, to the very end of the age."*

The church in Acts did exactly that; they preached and made disciples. Jesus instructed us to _____ the gospel and to
_____ our disciples what He taught us. The early church
did just that. It was this broader embracing of the Final Instruction
the Lord gave His Disciples that gave precedence to it becoming the
"Great Commission."

> *Acts 11:19-21 (NIV) "19 Now those who had been scattered by the*
> *persecution that broke out when Stephen was killed traveled as*
> *far as Phoenicia, Cyprus and Antioch, spreading the word only*
> *among Jews. 20 Some of them, however, men from Cyprus and*
> *Cyrene, went to Antioch and began to speak to Greeks also,*
> *telling them the good news about the Lord Jesus. 21 The Lord's*
> *hand was with them, and a great number of people believed*
> *and turned to the Lord."*

> *Acts 11:25-26 (NIV) 25 Then Barnabas went to Tarsus to look for*
> *Saul, 26 and when he found him, he brought him to Antioch. So*
> *for a whole year Barnabas and Saul met with the church and*
> *taught great numbers of people. The disciples were called*
> *Christians first at Antioch.*

We see this pattern replicated on many accounts in the Acts of the
Apostles. It is no wonder that the early church grew exponentially. I
believe, and see, that we will experience the same impact and transformation of nations as what the Apostles and the early church expe-
rienced when we embrace again, as the body of Christ, as Believers,
the **"Great Commission"** as our mission. We will cover the earth with
the Good News of Jesus Christ.

How will they believe without someone telling them?

Periodically we need to ask ourselves: ***How will they believe unless
_____ tell them?*** The answer to this question should always move us
to a commitment to act and share our faith.

> *Romans 10:14-15 (NIV) 14 How, then, can they call on the one they
> have not believed in? And how can they believe in the one of
> whom they have not heard? And how can they hear without
> someone preaching to them? 15 And how can they preach unless
> they are sent? As it is written, "How beautiful are the feet of
> those who bring good news!"*

Jesus modelled preaching and discipling

Jesus started His earthly ministry by doing exactly that; He preached
a Message of Repentance everywhere he went. John the Baptist also
started His ministry by preaching. The Apostles did the same. It is no
wonder that they were able to reach their entire world with the
Gospel since they went out, preached, and bore witness, and discipled the new Believers.

> *Matthew 3:1-2 (NIV) "1 In those days John the Baptist came,
> preaching in the wilderness of Judea 2 and saying, 'Repent, for
> the kingdom of heaven has come near.'"*

> *Matthew 4:17 (NIV) "17 From that time on Jesus began to preach,
> 'Repent, for the kingdom of heaven has come near.'"*

As a result of this preaching Jesus found His first Disciples. We
see this process modelled by Jesus in the Gospel of Luke. First Jesus
preached, and then performed a miracle, and then Peter bowed his
knees to Jesus and followed Him to be His Disciple.

Luke 5:1 (NIV) "1 One day as Jesus was standing by the Lake of Gennesaret, the people were crowding around him and listening to the word of God."

Jesus preached the Word of God next to the Lake of Gennesaret. It is here that He met Peter, Andrew, James and John, the owners of two fishing trawlers.

Luke 5:4-6 (NIV) "4 When he had finished speaking, he said to Simon, 'Put out into deep water, and let down the nets for a catch.' 5 Simon answered, 'Master, we've worked hard all night and haven't caught anything. But because you say so, I will let down the nets.' 6 When they had done so, they caught such a large number of fish that their nets began to break."

Jesus performed a miracle that astounded them. One of the consistent elements we witness in the work of the early church was their passionate obedience to _____ Jesus, *"perform miracles, signs and wonders,"* and _____. In the midst of severe persecution, the church advanced and even won the hostile Roman Empire.

Luke 5:8-9 (NIV) "8 When Simon Peter saw this, he fell at Jesus' knees and said, 'Go away from me, Lord; I am a sinful man!' 9 For he and all his companions were astonished at the catch of fish they had taken."

On a number of occasions, we see this same pattern of ministry replicated as well; Preach, miracles, repentance and people becoming Followers.

Luke 5:10-11 (NIV) 10 "...Then Jesus said to Simon, 'Don't be afraid; from now on you will fish for people.' 11 So they pulled their boats up on shore, left everything and followed him."

These first Disciples of the Lord witnesses firsthand a miracle, the impact of which impacted them so much that Peter fell to his knees and _____ that he was a sinner. The impact of us **preaching** or speaking the Word of God should result in people putting their faith in Jesus.

Peter preached, performed miracles and discipled wherever he went

The Apostle Peter was such an example of practicing this Spiritual Discipline right from the onset of the Church's Foundation. He is the one who stood up in the Day of Pentecost and preached that message that saw 3000 people coming to Christ.

> *Acts 2:14 (NIV) Peter Addresses the Crowd "14 Then Peter stood up with the Eleven, raised his voice and addressed the crowd: 'Fellow Jews and all of you who live in Jerusalem, let me explain this to you; listen carefully to what I say.'"*

Peter preached Jesus.

> *Acts 2:22 (NIV) "22 'Fellow Israelites, listen to this: Jesus of Nazareth was a man accredited by God to you by miracles, wonders and signs, which God did among you through him, as you yourselves know.'"*

His message included the death and resurrection of Jesus.

> *Acts 2:31-33 (NIV) 31 Seeing what was to come, he spoke of the resurrection of the Messiah, that he was not abandoned to the realm of the dead, nor did his body see decay. 32 God has raised this Jesus to life, and we are all witnesses of it. 33 Exalted to the right hand of God, he has received from the Father the*

promised Holy Spirit and has poured out what you now see and hear."

No preaching is complete unless it culminates in an opportunity or a call to _____ and to _____ Christ as Lord. The Lord's Hand will be upon the hearers to bring the conviction, but we have to follow through by leading them to Salvation.

This is exactly what transpired when Peter preached that incredible message on the Day of Pentecost. The people came under such a conviction that they actually asked Peter: "**What shall we do?**" They wanted to be saved. They wanted to be reconciled with God. They wanted to receive this Jesus into their lives.

> *Acts 2:36-41 (NIV) 36 "Therefore let all Israel be assured of this: God has made this Jesus, whom you crucified, both Lord and Messiah." 37 When the people heard this, they were cut to the heart and said to Peter and the other apostles, "Brothers, what shall we do?" 38 Peter replied, "Repent and be baptized, every one of you, in the name of Jesus Christ for the forgiveness of your sins. And you will receive the gift of the Holy Spirit. 39 The promise is for you and your children and for all who are far off—for all whom the Lord our God will call." 40 With many other words he warned them; and he pleaded with them, "Save yourselves from this corrupt generation." 41 Those who accepted his message were baptized, and about three thousand were added to their number that day"*

On many other occasions we see the same pattern of witnessing being followed; miracles, preaching and people putting their faith in Jesus Christ.

In the Acts of the Apostles, chapter three, we read about the Lame Beggar being healed, which was followed with an opportunity to share about Jesus of Nazareth. 5000 people came to the Lord as a result of that witnessing about the Lord Jesus being the Resurrected Christ and Messiah.

> *Acts 3:9-10 (NIV) "9 When all the people saw him walking and praising God, 10 they recognized him as the same man who used to sit begging at the temple gate called Beautiful, and they were filled with wonder and amazement at what had happened to him."*

The focus of his message was clear: repent, that your sins might be wiped out, and that times of refreshing might come.

> *Acts 3:19 (NIV) "19 Repent, then, and turn to God, so that your sins may be wiped out, that times of refreshing may come from the Lord,"*

The impact of the Lord working with Peter as He brought witness of the Lord Jesus was incredible. First the Sadducees and Teachers of the Law was infuriated by Peter and John's message on the Resurrection of Jesus Christ that they imprisoned them, but the impact of the message was so powerful that 5000 people believed the message. Secondly, Peter and John, after imprisonment, came out even stronger and continued in the work of the Lord.

> *Acts 4:2 (NIV) "2 They were greatly disturbed because the apostles were teaching the people, proclaiming in Jesus the resurrection of the dead."*

> *Acts 4:4 (NIV) "4 But many who heard the message believed; so the number of men who believed grew to about five thousand."*

The undeniable impact was clear to everyone in Jerusalem and beyond. More and more people believed in the Lord, both as a result of them seeing the demonstration of the Power of God, as well as hearing the Message that was delivered by the Apostles.

Acts 5:12 (NIV) The Apostles Heal Many "12 The apostles performed many signs and wonders among the people. And all the believers used to meet together in Solomon's Colonnade."

Acts 5:14-15 (NIV) 14 Nevertheless, more and more men and women believed in the Lord and were added to their number. 15 As a result, people brought the sick into the streets and laid them on beds and mats so that at least Peter's shadow might fall on some of them as he passed by.

The early Believers also preached everywhere

The early Believers spread the Word of God everywhere they went. The Gospel was preached everywhere. Preaching is bringing the message that Jesus is the Son of God, and by faith in Him as your Lord and Saviour, He can save you.

Acts 8:4 (NIV) "4 Those who had been scattered preached the word wherever they went."

As these Believers went, they preached, both to Jews and Gentiles.

Acts 11:19-21 (NIV) "19 Now those who had been scattered by the persecution that broke out when Stephen was killed traveled as far as Phoenicia, Cyprus and Antioch, spreading the word only among Jews. 20 Some of them, however, men from Cyprus and Cyrene, went to Antioch and began to speak to Greeks also, telling them the good news about the Lord Jesus. 21 The Lord's hand was with them, and a great number of people believed and turned to the Lord."

We see how the Words of Jesus came into fulfillment through these Believers, as they became witnesses in Judea, Samaria and into the ends of the earth. Here we have an account of them preaching to Greeks and later on to Samaritans as well.

Philip preached to the Samaritans.

Philip was one of the Believers who got scattered through the persecution that broke out in Jerusalem. Instead of shrinking back, they went and spread the Gospel everywhere, even to the Samaritans, which was totally cross-cultural for them at that time.

> Acts 8:5 (NIV) "5 Philip went down to a city in Samaria and proclaimed the Messiah there."

> Acts 8:12 (NIV) "12 But when they believed Philip as he proclaimed the good news of the kingdom of God and the name of Jesus Christ, they were baptized, both men and women."

> Acts 8:25 (NIV) "25 After they had further proclaimed the word of the Lord and testified about Jesus, Peter and John returned to Jerusalem, preaching the gospel in many Samaritan villages."

Paul immediately started preaching when he got saved

The Apostle Paul, when He came to the Lord, immediately started preaching and proving that Jesus was the Messiah.

> Acts 9:20 (NIV) "20 At once he began to preach in the synagogues that Jesus is the Son of God."

It is this obedient acting on the *"Great Commission"* that changed the entire world for Jesus.

In Acts Chapter 16 we see another example of the impact of *preaching* the Gospel and *Witnessing* for the Lord Jesus. After Paul had his *Macedonian Vision* him and his companions set out for Macedonia to preach the Good News of Jesus.

Acts 16:10 (NIV) "10 After Paul had seen the vision, we got ready at once to leave for Macedonia, concluding that God had called us to preach the gospel to them."

The result of Paul sharing the message of Christ was that, ***"The Lord opened her heart to respond to Paul's message."***

Acts 16:13-14 (NIV) "13 On the Sabbath we went outside the city gate to the river, where we expected to find a place of prayer. We sat down and began to speak to the women who had gathered there. 14 One of those listening was a woman from the city of Thyatira named Lydia, a dealer in purple cloth. She was a worshiper of God. The Lord opened her heart to respond to Paul's message."

What we learn from the *"Witnessing"* through the lives of the Apostles, and the Believers in Acts, are that they *"preached"* everywhere and that, *"the Lord"* truly *"**worked with them to confirm the Word**"*.

Conclusion

We are therefore required to make a commitment to witness by sharing our faith, preach and testify to what God did for us.

Assimilation Sheet for
INTRODUCTION TO SHARING OUR FAITH

1. Complete the statement. *Witnessing requires a commitment to both be a "_____" and "_____."*

2. Which Scripture teaches us this principle? _____

3. Complete the statement. *Witnessing requires a commitment to "_____" the Good News.*

4. Which Scripture teaches us this principle? _____

5. Complete the statement. *Witnessing requires a commitment to both "preach" and "_____."*

6. Which Scripture teaches us this principle? _____

7. How will the Gospel spread? _____
_____

8. What Scripture encourages us in this? _____

9. What did Jesus model to us regarding how to minister? *He was _____ and _____*

10. Which Scripture teaches us this principle? _____

11. What was one of the outcomes of Jesus' preaching in Luke chapter five? _____

12. What was the key things that happened when Jesus preached in Luke 5 verses 1-11? _____
_____

13. What did Peter do on the Day of Pentecost? _____

14. How many people came to the Lord as a result of this preaching? _____

15. What did Peter do in Acts chapter 3 verses 9 and onwards?
_____
_____

16. What was His main message? Give a verse. _____
_____

17. Where did the early Believers preach? Substantiate with Scriptures. _____
_____

. . .

18. Which Believer preached to the Samaritans? Substantiate with Scriptures. _____

19. What did Paul do when he got saved? Substantiate with Scriptures. _____

20. Paul delivered a message in Acts chapter sixteen in Macedonia. What was the impact of their sharing? Substantiate with Scripture. _____
_____

21. What did the Lord do when they preached the Word?

_____
_____

2

SHARING OUR FAITH IN A PRACTICAL WAY

SESSION TWO

In this session we will look at ways in which we can share our faith in a practical way.

How can we share our faith in a practical way?

1. Make the _____ **your life's mission.**

This means that you commit to embrace all the different aspects of the Great Commission and fulfill it daily. It is the most natural thing for new Believers to share their newfound faith in Jesus. I encourage you to make this a lifelong mission and discipline of yours to share your faith with others.

Make a commitment to this Mission. It requires:

- A commitment to "_____."
- That we "_____" the Gospel.
- That we "_____" those who accept Christ.
- That we "_____" the new Believers to obey everything Jesus taught us.

**2. Make a commitment to put on the "_____"
to share your faith.**

We are encouraged to put on the "**Full Armour of God**" daily. One of
the essential parts of the "**Armour of God**" is the "*Shoes of
_____*". Being prepared brings within us an expec-
tation to keep our eyes open for when the opportunity arises.

Being prepared also makes us less anxious when we have an
opportunity to share. Being prepared also makes us also bolder and
more confident since we expect to see how the Lord will open their
hearts to receive Him as their Lord and Savior.

> *Ephesians 6:15 (NIV)* "*15 and with your feet fitted with the readiness
> that comes from the gospel of peace.*"

> *Ephesians 6:15 (BBE)* "*15 Be ready with the good news of peace as
> shoes on your feet;*"

Our preparation for each day should include a readiness to share
the Hope we have in Jesus, whilst attending to keep our good
behavior.

> *1 Peter 3:15-16 (NIV 1984)* "*15 But in your hearts set apart Christ as
> Lord. Always be prepared to give an answer to everyone who
> asks you to give the reason for the hope that you have. But do
> this with gentleness and respect, 16 keeping a clear conscience,
> so that those who speak maliciously against your good behavior
> in Christ may be ashamed of their slander.*"

3. Learn how to share the Gospel like the Apostles did?

One of the top reasons why people do not share their faith, according
to research by Lesli White from Beliefnet.com[1], is that people "*don't
feel that they are knowledgeable*" to share the Gospel.

Let us look at the Gospel message.

THE GOSPEL

The strategy and content that the Apostles, and first Believers, used to share the Gospel is well noted in the New Testament. It was Biblically founded and intentionally pursued under the Power of the Holy Spirit. They used the Word of God in almost every account of witnessing about Jesus, and strongly depended on the Holy Spirit to bring conviction, and on the Lord to confirm His Word through Signs and Wonders. They pleaded with the listeners to be reconciled with God, to repent of their sins, and to accept Jesus Christ as Lord.

The Apostle Paul, in his address to the Church in Corinth, reminds them of the Gospel message by which they were saved:

> *1 Corinthians 15:1-8 (NIV) 1 Now, brothers, **I want to remind you of the gospel I preached to you**, which you received and on which you have taken your stand. 2 **By this gospel you are saved**, if you hold firmly to the word, I preached to you. Otherwise, you have believed in vain. 3 For what I received I passed on to you as of first importance : **that Christ died for our sins according to the Scriptures, 4 that he was buried, that he was raised on the third day according to the Scriptures, 5 and that he appeared** to Peter, and then to the Twelve. 6 After that, he appeared to more than five hundred of the brothers at the same time, most of whom are still living, though some have fallen asleep. 7 Then he appeared to James, then to all the apostles, 8 and last of all he appeared to me also, as to one abnormally born."*

The Gospel is about Jesus Christ, who _____ *for our sins, in our place, to save us, but then* _____ *from the dead and is* _____. We now serve the living God! The validation of the Scriptures is remarkable throughout this message and throughout the preaching of Jesus, His Disciples and the numerous accounts of where we read of the Believers preaching.

1. Christ died for our sins, according to the Scriptures.

Christ died for our sins when we were still dead in our sins. We all sinned and need a Savior. Christ is our Savior.

> *Isaiah 53:5 (NIV) "5 But he was pierced for our transgressions, he was crushed for our iniquities; the punishment that brought us peace was upon him, and by his wounds we are healed."*

He was wounded for our transgressions. He is also the Lamb of God who took away our sins by becoming the sacrificial Lamb to satisfy the requirement of God for the remission of sins.

> *John 1:29 (NIV) "29 The next day John saw Jesus coming toward him and said, "Look, the Lamb of God, who takes away the sin of the world!"*

Christ, the Righteous, died in our place. We deserved to die, but Christ took our place on the Cross.

> *1 Peter 2:24 (NIV) "24 He himself bore our sins in his body on the tree, so that we might die to sins and live for righteousness; by his wounds you have been healed."*

2. Christ rose from the dead to offer us a living hope and eternal life.

We believe that Christ was buried, and then rose from the dead. He is alive and offers eternal life to all who believe in Him. We live this life for Him so that we will live with Him for eternity.

> *1 Corinthians 15:19-20, 22 (NIV) 19 If only for this life we have hope in Christ, we are to be pitied more than all men. 20 But Christ has indeed been raised from the dead, the firstfruits of those*

who have fallen asleep. 22 For as in Adam all die, so in Christ
all will be made alive.

Eternal life can only be offered by One who rose from the dead.
Christ rose from the dead and therefore He offers eternal life to all
who believe in Him.

> *John 3:16 (NIV) 16 "For God so loved the world that he gave his one*
> *and only Son, that whoever believes in him shall not perish but*
> *have eternal life."*

> *John 6:40 (NIV) "40 For my Father's will is that everyone who*
> *looks to the Son and believes in him shall have eternal life, and I*
> *will raise him up at the last day."*

3. Christ is coming back again to take us to be with Him forever.

Jesus is coming back! He is coming back to bring us to be with Him
forever. He is also coming to reward us for our walk in Him. We will
all stand before Him, some to receive their eternal reward and some
to be sent into eternal damnation.

> *Matthew 16:27 (NIV) "27 For the Son of Man is going to come in his*
> *Father's glory with his angels, and then he will reward each*
> *person according to what he has done."*

Jesus Himself said that He is coming back again. In this Scripture
He says that He is returning as the "Rewarder." Jesus also taught that
when He returns, He will take us back with Him to be with Him
forever. We live with this hope in our hearts always. We have a living
Hope.

> *John 14:3 (NIV) "3 And if I go and prepare a place for you, I will*
> *come back and take you to be with me that you also may be*
> *where I am."*

The Apostle Paul said in his letter, to the church in Thessalonica, that when Jesus returns, that we who are still alive will meet Him in the air, and be with Him forever. This is something to look forward to.

> *1 Thessalonians 4:16-17 (NIV) "16 For the Lord himself will come down from heaven, with a loud command, with the voice of the archangel and with the trumpet call of God, and the dead in Christ will rise first. 17 After that, we who are still alive and are left will be caught up together with them in the clouds to meet the Lord in the air. And so we will be with the Lord forever."*

4. We receive Him as Lord by confessing our sins and ask Him to be our Lord.

The Bible teaches us that His blood washes and cleanses us. We are saved when we confess our sins and confess Jesus as the Lord of our lives. The Bible teaches us in 1 John chapter one that we receive forgiveness when we repent and confess our sins. The Lord purifies us from all our wrongdoings.

> 1 John 1:9 (NIV) 9 If we confess our sins, he is faithful and just and will forgive us our sins and purify us from all unrighteousness.

The Bible also teaches that when we openly *"confess Jesus as the Lord"* of our lives and simultaneously believe in our hearts that God raised Him from the dead, that we will be saved.

> *Romans 10:9 (NIV) "9 That if you confess with your mouth, 'Jesus is Lord,' and believe in your heart that God raised him from the dead, you will be saved."*

Peter concluded his message on the Day of Pentecost with a Call to Repentance.

Acts 2:38 (NIV) "38 Peter replied, 'Repent and be baptized, every one of you, in the name of Jesus Christ for the forgiveness of your sins. And you will receive the gift of the Holy Spirit.'"

Jesus Himself taught this Gospel message to His Disciples.

Luke 24:46-47 (NIV) 46 He told them, "This is what is written: The Christ will suffer and rise from the dead on the third day, 47 and repentance and forgiveness of sins will be preached in his name to all nations, beginning at Jerusalem."

A Note to remember when we present the Gospel Message:

The Gospel Message should be encased by the _____ of God

Whenever Jesus preached, He referenced the Word of God. When Peter stood up on the Day of Pentecost and delivered that first Gospel Message, it was encased in Scriptural references. Twice in the first message he referenced the Scriptures.

Acts 2:14, 16 (NIV) "14 Then Peter stood up with the Eleven, raised his voice and addressed the crowd: 'Fellow Jews and all of you who live in Jerusalem, let me explain this to you; listen carefully to what I say. 16 No, this is what was spoken by the prophet Joel:'"

Acts 2:25 (NIV) "25 David said about him: 'I saw the Lord always before me. Because he is at my right hand, I will not be shaken.'"

When Peter and John spoke in the Colonnade of Solomon when Peter healed the cripple man, he encased it in references to Moses and the Prophets.

Acts 3:22-23 (NIV) "22 For Moses said, 'The Lord your God will raise up for you a prophet like me from among your own people; you must listen to everything he tells you. 23 Anyone who does not listen to him will be completely cut off from among his people.'"

Acts 3:24-25 (NIV) 24 "Indeed, all the prophets from Samuel on, as many as have spoken, have foretold these days. 25 And you are heirs of the prophets and of the covenant God made with your fathers. He said to Abraham, 'Through your offspring all peoples on earth will be blessed.'"

When Peter and John were brought before the Sanhedrin because of their preaching and the healing miracle of the cripple man, Peter referenced the Scriptures

Acts 4:10-12 (NIV) "10 then know this, you and all the people of Israel: It is by the name of Jesus Christ of Nazareth, whom you crucified but whom God raised from the dead, that this man stands before you healed. 11 He is "'the stone you builders rejected, which has become the capstone.'12 Salvation is found in no one else, for there is no other name under heaven given to men by which we must be saved.'"

When Stephen spoke in Acts 7, he referenced the Word of God throughout his message. When Philip spoke to the Eunuch when the Holy Spirit directed him to go there, the Message was encased in Scripture.

The word of God is truly "_____" and "_____" and able to work Powerfully in us. The more we allow it on our lips we unlock its Power to bring change and transformation in the lives of people around us.

∼

The Gospel should be centered on Jesus Christ as the _____ of God.

Whenever the Apostles and first Believers preached and shared the Gospel it was always centered on Jesus Christ. The whole Gospel centers on the Salvatory Work of Jesus Christ on the cross of Calvary. It's not about you or me; it's about Jesus, and us putting our faith in Him.

> *Acts 2:22-24 (NIV) "22 "Men of Israel, listen to this: Jesus of Nazareth was a man accredited by God to you by miracles, wonders and signs, which God did among you through him, as you yourselves know.23 This man was handed over to you by God's set purpose and foreknowledge; and you, with the help of wicked men, put him to death by nailing him to the cross. 24 But God raised him from the dead, freeing him from the agony of death, because it was impossible for death to keep its hold on him."*

> *Acts 2:32-33 (NIV) "32 God has raised this Jesus to life, and we are all witnesses of the fact. 33 Exalted to the right hand of God, he has received from the Father the promised Holy Spirit and has poured out what you now see and hear."*

At every juncture Peter, and the other Believers, witnessed about Jesus as the Resurrected Christ.

> *Acts 3:16 (NIV) "16 By faith in the name of Jesus, this man whom you see and know was made strong. It is Jesus' name and the faith that comes through him that has given this complete healing to him, as you can all see."*

> *Acts 3:18-20 (NIV) "18 But this is how God fulfilled what he had foretold through all the prophets, saying that his Christ would suffer. 19 Repent, then, and turn to God, so that your sins may*

*be wiped out, that times of refreshing may come from the Lord,
20 and that he may send the Christ, who has been appointed
for you–even Jesus."*

The Gospel message is received by putting our _____ in Jesus as Lord

The Gospel is received by confession, and by faith, in receiving Christ as Lord.

> *Romans 10:9-10 (NIV) 9 That if you confess with your mouth,
> "Jesus is Lord," and believe in your heart that God raised him
> from the dead, you will be saved. 10 For it is with your heart
> that you believe and are justified, and it is with your mouth
> that you confess and are saved.*

> *Romans 10:13 (NIV) "13 for, "Everyone who calls on the name of the
> Lord will be saved."*

The preaching of the Gospel was always, and should always be accompanied by a strong sense of _____ on the hearers.

When Peter stood up in the midst of the Twelve and preached on the Day of Pentecost, a deep conviction came on all those who heard the Word of God. It was this same strong conviction that accompanied their messages in the Synagogue and wherever they preached the Word. The Word of God is Living and active. The Gospel is the Power of God to change lives.

> *Acts 2:37-40 (NIV) 37 When the people heard this, they were cut to
> the heart and said to Peter and the other apostles, "Brothers,
> what shall we do?" 38 Peter replied, "Repent and be baptized,
> every one of you, in the name of Jesus Christ for the forgiveness
> of your sins. And you will receive the gift of the Holy Spirit. 39
> The promise is for you and your children and for all who are far*

*off–for all whom the Lord our God will call." 40 With many
other words he warned them; and he pleaded with them, "Save
yourselves from this corrupt generation.""*

*Acts 11:21 (NIV) "21 The Lord's hand was with them, and a great
number of people believed and turned to the Lord."*

When Paul wrote to the Church in Thessalonica, he reminded
them of how they received the Gospel. They received it; **"with deep
conviction"**.

*1 Thessalonians 1:4-5 (NIV) "4 For we know, brothers loved by God,
that he has chosen you, 5 because our gospel came to you not
simply with words, but also with power, with the Holy Spirit
and with deep conviction. You know how we lived among you
for your sake."*

Conclusion

When we keep these essentials of the Gospel message in the forefront
of our hearts, we will see tremendous results, since the Gospel is the
Power of God to change lives.

Romans 1:16 (NIV) 16 For I am not ashamed of the gospel,
because it is the power of God that brings salvation to
everyone who believes: first to the Jew, then to the Gentile.

We will do well to encase the Gospel message with the Truth of
the Word. We will do well to always focus our message on the work of
Christ on the Cross, and that He is the returning Resurrected Christ.

Assimilation Sheet for
Sharing our faith in a Practical way.

1. Complete the sentence. *Make the "_____"* *your life's mission.*

2. Complete the sentence and provide a Scripture. *Make a commitment to put on the "_____ of preparedness" to share your faith.* _____

3. Provide a Scriptural basis for sharing the Gospel.

_____

4. Share the Gospel Message briefly, and provide substantiating Scriptures for each point:

a. _____

_____

b. _____

_____

c. _____

_____

d. _____

_____

5. Complete the sentence. *The Gospel Message should be encased by the* _____ *of God.* Why do we do this? Give at least one example.

_____

_____

6. Give at least one other reason for using the Word of God in presenting the Gospel Message. _____

_____

_____

7. Complete the sentence. *The Gospel should be centered on Jesus Christ as the* _____ *of God.*

8. Which Scripture exhorts you most to present the gospel in this way? _____

_____

_____

9. How do we receive Christ in our hearts? Provide a Scripture.

_____

_____

_____

10. Complete the sentence and provide at least one Scriptural reference. *The preaching of the Gospel was always, and should always be, accompanied by a strong sense of* _____ *on the hearers.*

_____

11. What does the message in Romans 1 verse 16 encourage in?

_____

_____

3

THE PRACTICAL GOSPEL MESSAGE

SESSION THREE

H*ere is an easy to remember way of sharing the Gospel:*

*"Every conversation starts with an opener. We say: "**Hi, How are you?**" Or "**How's your day going?**" Or, we make statements on the weather or current affairs to engage in a conversation. It is no different for us when we start the actual presentation of the Gospel message, it starts with an opener, assuming of course that you established a platform from which you already engaged the person and are now ready to share Christ with them."*

1. Opener

How are you? How are things going nowadays? Do you know Jesus Christ? Can I tell you about Him?

"Remember, the Gospel is all about people putting their faith in Jesus Christ. It's not about them, or about you, it's about Jesus. You desire to reconcile them to God through faith in Jesus. The moment we start witnessing about Christ, the Power of God, to save people, is activated, and

God starts working with you to open their hearts to save them. God needs a Messenger and the moment you become His Messenger, the Holy Spirit and Jesus start doing their part to bring conviction to save the hearers. You are delivering this message to implore people on Christ behalf to be reconciled to God."

*2 Corinthians 5:18-20 (NIV) 18 All this is from God, who reconciled us to himself through Christ and **gave us the ministry of reconciliation:** 19 that God was reconciling the world to himself in Christ, not counting people's sins against them. And **he has committed to us the message of reconciliation.** 20 We are therefore Christ's ambassadors, as though God were making his appeal through us. **We implore you on Christ's behalf: Be reconciled to God.***

The Bible message is clear: **Be reconciled to God!**

How can we be _____ to God?

We have to be reconciled to come into a relationship with Jesus, but we need to first understand our standing and relationship with God. Most of us did not even know that we were lost without Him.

2. Man

Mankind is like sheep without a Shepherd. Mankind find themselves caught in their sins. Many pursue things that make them have a sense of feeling alive, but truly trying to deal with the sense of being empty and looking to find the purpose for existence.

It is like loving someone: until they find a place in your heart, the relationship remains without meaning or purpose. We were created to live in fellowship with God, however, our sins separated us from God.

∾

*Isaiah 59:1-4 (NIV) 1 Surely the arm of the LORD is not too short to save, nor his ear too dull to hear. 2 But **your iniquities have separated you from your God;** your sins have hidden his face from you, so that he will not hear. 3 For your hands are stained with blood, your fingers with guilt. Your lips have spoken falsely, and your tongue mutters wicked things. 4 No one calls for justice; no one pleads a case with integrity. They rely on empty arguments, they utter lies; they conceive trouble and give birth to evil.*

Many people live unfulfilled lives, having a sense of feeling empty on the inside, even though they might seem successful and fulfilled to others. The reason for this is found in the Bible: *Our sinful lives deprive us of the glorious in-dwelt presence and Glory of God.* Until we give Jesus His rightful place in our lives, we will always have a void that could only be filled by Him. Every person on the planet live with this void and separation within them.

Romans 3:23 (NIV) "23 for all have sinned and fall short of the glory of God"

All of us sinned and are dead in our sins. Adam and Eve sinned in Eden. Through their sin, sin and spiritual death came to all mankind. We are all Sinners and are in need of a Saviour who can save us from our sin and give us eternal life.

1 Corinthians 15:22 (NIV 1984) "22 For as in Adam all die, so in Christ all will be made alive."

Until we accept the gracious work of Christ, who already made provision in dealing with our sins, the void remains in us. This can change when we acknowledge God and His love for us.

3. God

God loves us so much that he sent His Son to pay the price to redeem us of our sins. He now offers Salvation to all who accept and believe in His Son.

> *John 3:16 (NIV)*
> *"16 For God so loved the world that he gave his one and only Son, that whoever believes in him shall not perish but have eternal life."*

God is a loving God who does not want to see anyone lost, or to perish in their sin. He desires to have a restored relationship with us.

> 1 Timothy 2:3-4 (NIV)
> 3 This is good, and pleases God our Savior, 4 who wants all people to be saved and to come to a knowledge of the truth.

God does not want to see anyone die in their sins. He would rather have us repent, turn to him, and live.

> Ezekiel 18:32 (NIV)
> 32 For I take no pleasure in the death of anyone, declares the Sovereign LORD. Repent and live!

> Ezekiel 33:11 (NIV)
> 11 Say to them, 'As surely as I live, declares the Sovereign LORD, I take no pleasure in the death of the wicked, but rather that they turn from their ways and live. Turn! Turn from your evil ways! Why will you die, people of Israel?'

What our loving God wants is for all mankind to come to repentance of their sins, and be saved by the blood of Jesus.

2 Peter 3:9 (NIV) 9 The Lord is not slow in keeping his promise, as some understand slowness. Instead he is patient with you, not wanting anyone to perish, but everyone to come to repentance.

This is only possible through His Son, Jesus Christ.

4. Jesus Christ

Who is Jesus Christ?

Jesus Christ is the Son of God, who was conceived by the Holy Spirit, and born of the Virgin Mary. He was crucified, and died for our sins, and was buried. On the third day He rose again, as victor over death, to give eternal life to all who would believe in Him.

> *Isaiah 53:5 (NIV) "5 But he was pierced for our transgressions, he was crushed for our iniquities; the punishment that brought us peace was upon him, and by his wounds we are healed."*

> *John 1:29 (NIV) "29 The next day John saw Jesus coming toward him and said, "Look, the Lamb of God, who takes away the sin of the world!"*

We appropriate this gracious work of Christ by putting our Faith in Jesus Christ to save us.

5. What we Believe

> *" Remember, we are asking them to put their faith in Jesus by the way we are presenting the Gospel. For this to remain authentic, we need to share with them why we have placed our faith in Jesus as well as declare what we believe. We need to make a confession of what believe."*

We believe that:

- Jesus is the Son of God
- He died on the Cross for our sins
- He rose again on the third day and is alive
- Forgiveness for our sins is only found in Him
- Only Jesus can save us and bring us back to a restored relationship with the Father.

"It is valuable that we declare our faith and what we believe. We are sharing our faith by declaring what we believe. We are witnessing when we declare our faith."

Here is a version of the **Apostles' Creed** to which we subscribe.

Apostles' Creed

I believe in God, the Father Almighty,
Creator of heaven and earth.
I believe in Jesus Christ, God's only Son, our Lord,
who was conceived by the Holy Spirit,
born of the Virgin Mary,
suffered under Pontius Pilate,
was crucified, died, and was buried;
He descended to the dead.
On the third day He rose again;
He ascended into heaven,
He is seated at the right hand of God, our Father,
And He will come to judge the living and the dead.
I believe in the Holy Spirit,
And I believe in one holy Christian and apostolic Church,
the communion of saints,
the forgiveness of sins,
the resurrection of the body,
and life everlasting, Amen.[1]

"They might ask you: **What must I do to believe in Jesus? How can I be saved from my sins?** *Or, we might ask them:* **Do you believe in Jesus?** *Either way, if they don't ask, you can ask them and then move on to the next point."*

6. Confession and Faith

We are saved when we confess our sins and confess our faith in Jesus Christ as Lord and Savior. God offered eternal life to all who would believe in His Son, Jesus Christ. When we repent of our sins, He forgives us and restores into a right relationship with God.

> *Romans 10:9-10 (NIV) "9 That if you confess with your mouth, 'Jesus is Lord,' and believe in your heart that God raised him from the dead, you will be saved. 10 For it is with your heart that you believe and are justified, and it is with your mouth that you confess and are saved."*

This verse in the Bible really sums it up beautifully: "**if** *we confess Jesus as Lord, and believe in our hearts that God raised Him from the dead*," we will be saved. This promise is available for everyone who calls on Jesus to be their Lord.

> *Romans 10:13 (NIV) 13 for, "Everyone who calls on the name of the Lord will be saved."*

The only thing that we need to do is repent of our sins, ask Him to be our Lord, and put our faith in Him.

> *Acts 2:38 (NIV) "38 Peter replied, 'Repent and be baptized, every one of you, in the name of Jesus Christ for the forgiveness of your sins. And you will receive the gift of the Holy Spirit.'"*

Jesus gave His Life to save us. He is standing at the door of our hearts, knocking. He wants to come into our lives.

Revelation 3:20 (NIV) 20 Here I am! I stand at the door and
knock. If anyone hears my voice and opens the door, I will
come in and eat with that person, and they with me.

I believe He is here right now, knocking at the door of your heart.

*"Once you shared with people on how to receive Jesus as their Lord and
Savior, you can ask if they want to accept Jesus, and then you can ask
them if you could lead them in a prayer for Salvation."*

We have this amazing promise from the Bible in John chapter
one, and it says that: We can become children of God when we
receive Jesus into our lives.

John 1:12-13 (NIV) 12 Yet to all who did receive him, to those
who believed in his name, he gave the right to become
children of God — 13 children born not of natural descent,
nor of human decision or a husband's will, but born
of God.

7. Ask

*"After sharing your faith, you need to give and opportunity for them to
respond to what you shared with them. This opportunity is presented by
asking a question or two. Sometimes, like in the Book of Acts when Peter
witnessed, the people will pause you to enquire as to How they may
receive Jesus. If they don't ask on their own, then give them an opportunity
to receive Jesus following their response to these questions. You need to ask
them:"*

**Do you want to open the door of your heart and ask Jesus into
your life?
May I lead you in a Prayer of confession, and to accept Jesus as
your Lord and Savior?**

"Now lead them in the following prayer of confession. Ask them to repeat the prayer after you. Pray the prayer, sentence by sentence, and let them repeat it after you."

8. Prayer

Father God in Heaven, I confess that I am a Sinner. I repent of my sins and ask for Your Forgiveness. Please forgive me, save me from my sin, and make me Your Child today. Wash me with Your Blood, Cleanse me by the Power of Your Holy Spirit. I ask You now to be my Lord and Savior. I ask you into my life. I ask this in the Name of Jesus. Amen

9. Congratulations

"Congratulate them on their decision to receive Jesus as the Lord of their lives."

- Affirm that Jesus accepted their confession of sins, according to 1 John 1 verse 9, and that
- He forgave them their sins.
- He washed them with His Blood.
- Affirm that they are now children of God.

"The essential concluding part of when people receive Jesus as their Lord and Saviour is the assurance that we need to give them that they are not alone, but that you will continue this journey with them, to help them as Followers of Jesus. This is what we have been praying for and trusting for: souls to be saved. Now that we see our prayers answered we can start phase two by getting them baptised and discipled."

Assimilation Sheet for
The Practical Gospel Message.

1. What do we use at the Beginning of our presentation? Give an example. *A.* _____ , *and B.* _____

_____

2. What is the second point in our practical Gospel Message?

_____

3. What message do we wish to convey about mankind? What Scripture can you use to substantiate your point? _____

_____

_____

4. What is the third point of our practical Gospel Message? Provide a Scripture. _____

_____

5. What is the fourth point of our practical Gospel Message? Provide a Scripture. _____

_____

_____

6. What is the fifth point of our practical Gospel Message?

_____

7. How can we conclude this point? _____

_____

8. What is the sixth point of our practical Gospel Message? Provide a Scripture. _____

_____

_____

9. We conclude this with the seventh point. _____

_____

_____

10. Write out the Prayer for Salvation. _____

_____

_____

11. How do we close our conversation? _____

_____

_____

_____

PART II

OTHER BOOKS BY DR. HENDRIK J VORSTER

OTHER BOOKS BY DR HENDRIK J VORSTER

Discipleship Foundations - Step One - Salvation Disciple Manual

Step One - Salvation

This Course explores the "How to" be Born Again and to establish a solid Foundation for your faith in Jesus Christ. It is based on Hebrews chapter 6 verses 1 and 2, and explores:

Repentance of dead works,

Faith in God,

Baptisms,

Laying on of hands,

Resurrection of the dead, and

Eternal Judgement

Teacher Manuals and Video Teaching material are available from our website: www.churchplantinginstitute.com

Discipleship Foundations Step Two - Values and Spiritual Disciplines Disciple Manual

Step Two - Values and Spiritual Disciplines Disciple Manual

This Course explores the "How to" develop spiritual disciplines as well as 52 Values Jesus taught. It is based on the teachings of Jesus to His Disciples, and explores:

Spiritual Disciplines

The disciplines we explore are: Reading, meditating on the Word of God, Prayer, Stewardship, Fasting, Servanthood, Simplicity, Worship, and Witnessing.

Values of the Kingdom of God

Humility, Mournfulness, meekness, Spiritual Passion, Mercifulness, Purity, Peacemaker, Patient endurance, Example, Custodian, Reconciliatory, Resoluteness, Loving, Discreetness, Forgiving, Kingdom of God Investor, God-minded, Kingdom of God prioritiser, Introspective, Persistent, Considerate, Conservative, Fruit-bearing, Practitioner, Accountability, Faithful, Childlikeness, Unity, Servanthood, Loyalty, Gratefulness, Stewardship, Obedience, Carefulness, Compassion, Caring, Confidence, Steadfastness, Contentment, Teachable, Deference, Diligence, Trustworthiness, Gentleness, Discernment, Truthfulness, Generous, Kindness, Watchfulness, Perseverance, Honouring and Submissive.

Teacher Manuals and Video Teaching material are available from our website: www.churchplantinginstitute.com

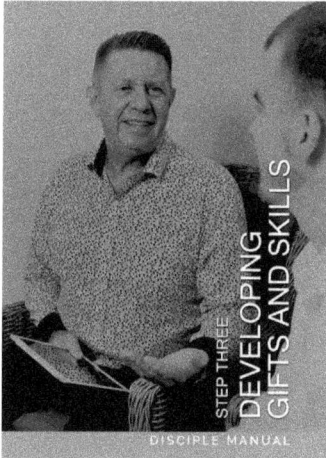

Discipleship Foundations Step Three - Developing Gifts and Skills

Step Three - Developing Gifts and Skills

This course is run through five weekend encounters. These weekend encounters have been designed to help Disciples discover their spiritual gifts, as well as learn skills to use their gifts, and to serve the Lord for the extension of His Kingdom. The Weekend Encounters are:

Gifts Discovery Weekend Encounter

We learn about Ministerial Office gifts, Service gifts, and Supernatural Spiritual Gifts. We discover our own, and then learn How we may use them to build up the local Church.

Survey of the Bible Weekend Encounter

During this weekend we do a survey of the Bible, from Genesis to Revelation. We also learn about the History of the Bible as well as How we can make most of our time in the Word.

Sharing your Faith Weekend Encounter

During this weekend we learn about the Gospel message, and How to share our faith effectively.

Overcoming Weekend Encounter

During this weekend we deal with those thistles and thorns that smother the growth and harvest of the good seed sown into our lives. We address How to overcome fear, unforgiveness, lust and the cares of the world with faith and obedience.

Shepherd Leader Weekend Encounter

During this weekend encounter we learn about being a Good Shepherd, and How to best disciple in a small group.

Teacher Manuals and Video Teaching material are available from our website: www.churchplantinginstitute.com

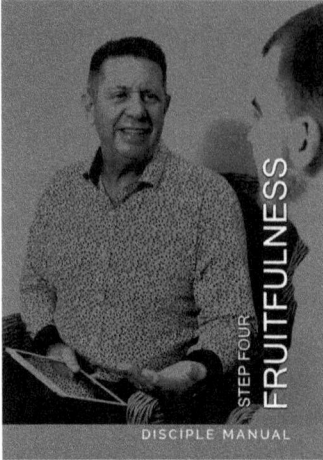

Discipleship Foundations Step Four - Fruitfulness

Step Four - Fruitfulness

We were saved to serve. This course has been designed to mobilise Believers from Learners to Practitioners. These sessions have been prepared for individual use with those who are producing fruit.

We explore:

1. Introduction.

2. Walking with purpose.

3. Build purposeful relationships. Finding Worthy Men

4. Priesthood. Praying effectively for those entrusted to you.

5. Caring compassionately.

6. Walking worthily.

7. Walking in the Spirit.

8. Practicing hospitality.

Teacher Manuals and Video Teaching material are available from our website: www.churchplantinginstitute.com

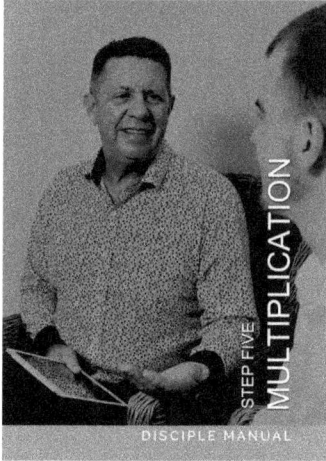

Discipleship Foundations Step Five - Multiplication

Step Five - Multiplication

This course was designed to assist fruit-producing disciples to live a life that will encourage a lifetime of fruitfulness. It will also give disciples skills and guidelines to navigate their disciples through seasons of challenge and growth. We explore:

1. Vision and dreams.

2. Set Godly Goals.

3. Character development

4. Gifts development

Impartation and Activation

5. Fruitfulness comes through constant challenge.

6. Relationships

Family, Children and Friends

7. The Power of encouragement

8. Finances

Personal and Ministry finances

9. Dealing with setbacks

- How to deal with failure?
- How to deal with betrayal?
- How to deal with rejection?
- How to deal with trials?
- How to deal with despondency?

10. Eternal rewards

Teacher Manuals and Video Teaching material are available from our website: www.churchplantinginstitute.com

VALUES
OF THE
KINGDOM
OF
GOD

Dr. Hendrik J. Vorster

Values of the Kingdom of God

By Dr. Hendrik J Vorster

Everyone desires to be known as a pleasant to be around with kind of person. This book helps you develop values towards such a godly character. This book explores 52 Values of the Kingdom of God.

Books are available from our website: www.churchplantinginstitute.com

SPIRITUAL
DISCIPLINES
OF THE
KINGDOM
OF
GOD

Spiritual Disciplines of the Kingdom of God

By Dr. Hendrik J Vorster

Every Believer desires to be a Fruit-producing branch in the Vineyard of our Lord. Developing spiritual disciplines is to develop spiritual roots from which our faith can draw sap to grow strong and fruit-bearing branches. This Book explores Nine Spiritual Disciplines of the Kingdom of God.

Books are available from our website: www.churchplantinginstitute.com

Church Planting
How to plant a dynamic church

Dr. Hendrik J. Vorster
Foreword by: Dr. Yonggi Cho

Church Planting - by Dr Hendrik J Vorster

Church Planting - How to plant a dynamic, disciple-making church
By Dr Hendrik J Vorster

This is a handbook for those who wish to plant a disciple-making church. This book explores every aspect of church planting, and is widely used in over 70 Nations on 6 Continents. Here is a list of the areas that are explored:

1. The challenge to plant New Churches
2. Phases of Church Planting
3. Phase One of Church Planting - The Calling, Vision and Preparation Phase
4. The Call to Church Planting
5. Twelve Characteristics of Church Planting Leaders
6. Church Planting Terminology
7. Phase Two of Church Planting - Discipleship
8. The Process of Discipleship
9. Phase Three of Church Planting - Congregating the Discipleship Groups
10. Understanding Church Planting Finances
11. Understanding Church staff
12. Phase Four of Church Planting - Ministry development and Church Launching Phase
13. Understanding and Implementing Systems
14. Phase Five of Church Planting - Multiplication
15. Understanding the challenges in Church Planting
16. How to succeed in Church Planting
17. How to plant a House Church

Student Manuals and Video Teaching material are available from our website: www.churchplantinginstitute.com

Discipleship Foundation Series on Video

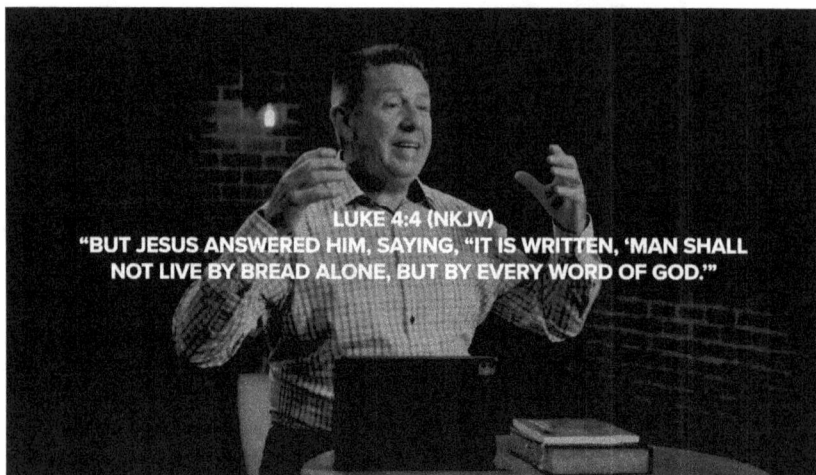

Dr. Vorster teaching via Video

185 Video Teachings are available for each of the Sessions taught throughout these Discipleship Courses.

Discipleship Foundation Series

We have Five, completely recorded, Discipleship Courses available on Video at www.discipleshipcourses.com

- **Step One - Salvation** (*This 7-week course helps the new Believer to establish, and build a solid Foundation for their faith to build on.*) This course is available, **without charge**, upon free registration.
- **Step Two - Values and Spiritual Disciplines** (*This 9-week Course helps the young Believer to put down Spiritual Roots, by establishing spiritual disciplines, and by learning the values of the Kingdom of God.*)
- **Step Three - Developing Gifts and Skills** (*This Course is usually presented during 5 Weekend Encounters, or over a 23-week period. We explore Spiritual Gifts and How to use them*

to build up the local Church. We **explore the Bible**, and its origins, during one part to ensure we build our lives on the Handbook of the Bible. We also learn **How to share our faith.** We learn **How to deal with Strongholds** that might hold us back in fulfilling God's purpose. And finally, we learn **How to best Mentor** those whom we lead to Christ.)

- **Step Four - Discipling Fruit-Producers** (*During this 8-week course* we learn How to teach our Disciples the principles that will develop, and maintain, fruitfulness.)
- **Step Five - Multiplication** (*During this 11-week Course we learn How to Mentor our Leaders to lead strong and healthy Fruit-producers.*)

Free registration for access to these Video resources is available at www.dicipleshipcourses.com

Church Planting Training Videos

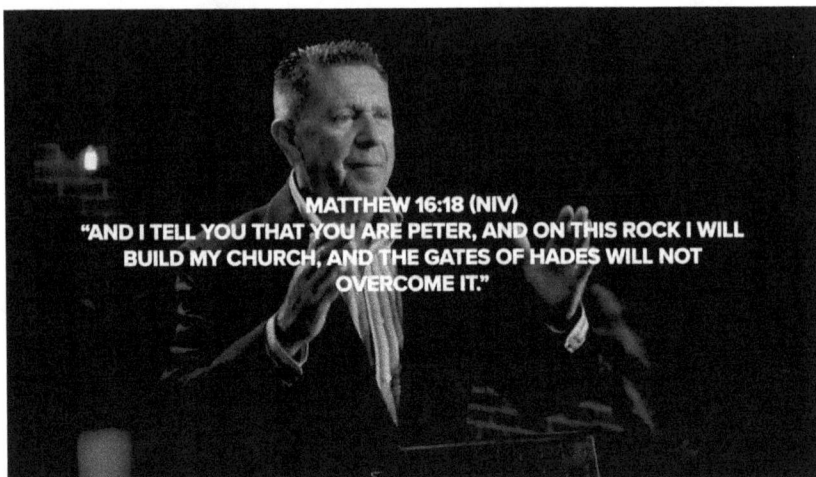

Dr. Vorster teaching via Video

42 Video Teachings are available in this **Church Planting Course.**

- Introduction to Church Planting
- Why plant New Churches?
- Phases of Church Planting Overview
- Phase 1 - Preparation Phase
- Phase 2 - Team Building Phase
- Phase 3 - Prelaunch Phase
- Phase 4 - Launch Phase
- Phase 5 - Multiplication Phase
- Church Planting Trials
- Next Steps

Free Enrolment is available at www.churchplantingcourses.com

Advanced Coaching sessions are available for those who enrolled in the Masters Training Program.

ENDNOTES

2. Sharing Our Faith In A Practical Way

1. https://www.beliefnet.com/faiths/christianity/galleries/7-reasons-christians-dont-share-their-faith.

3. The Practical Gospel Message

1. https://en.wikipedia.org/wiki/Apostles%27_Creed

www.ingramcontent.com/pod-product-compliance
Lightning Source LLC
Chambersburg PA
CBHW070459050426
42449CB00012B/3041

9 781955 923156